T0267158

AUSTRALIAN
BIRDS
IN PICTURES

AUSTRALIAN
BIRDS
IN PICTURES

Matthew Jones and Duade Paton

Tribute to Matt

The completion of this book is a tribute to Matthew Jones who left this earth all too soon in 2018.

Matt's love of and connection to the natural world was unfathomable. His unique perspective saw the interrelatedness of things and inspired many to view nature in a different way. Matt had the courage, perseverance and compassion to dedicate his life to doing what he could to protect it. The photos in this book are his final gift to humanity. It is hoped that people will be in awe of the beauty and diversity of Australian birds and that we can work together to protect them and their habitats not only for their own sake, but for ours too. Thank you Duade Paton for your photographic contribution and completing this book in honour of Matt's wild spirit.

Previous spread:
Eastern Curlew
Numenius madagascariensis
SHOALHAVEN HEADS, NEW SOUTH WALES

This 'Endangered' species uses its unbelievably long bill to probe into tidal mudflats and clasp onto any prey it finds. It has evolved to be able to reach further into the mud than any other shorebird, allowing it to access prey that is out of reach to others.

Following spread:
Scarlet-chested Parrot
Neophema splendida
GLUEPOT RESERVE, SOUTH AUSTRALIA

This species is surely one of the most striking looking birds in Australia. It is a nomadic traveller of inland Australia, following flowering plants and locating areas with abundant food. This makes it a very difficult bird to track and photograph. Both parents share duties in the rearing of the chicks, delivering food on a regular basis.

CONTENTS

INTRODUCTION

Australia has some of the most diverse and beautiful
birdlife found anywhere on the planet. Due to the
country's geographical isolation, Australian birds
evolved into an array of colourful, fascinating
and often utterly unique forms. With more than
800 regularly occurring species occupying every
possible niche and habitat, plus another 150 or so
rare visitors, Australia has almost 10 per cent of
the world's bird species. Of these, more than 350
species are endemic, meaning that they are not found
anywhere else in the world.

Australian Birds in Pictures is a celebration of
Australia's unique avifauna through visually engaging
and wonderful photos. The images capture birds
in their natural environments, showcasing their
behaviours and the features that help make them
unique. The two authors have spent many years in the
field, which has led to a deep understanding of bird

behaviour. This skill has led to the authors capturing some genuinely remarkable and perhaps never to be repeated images.

The book has been divided into twelve chapters which cover an array of different behaviours and habitats, from colourful parrots to the fascinating breeding displays of bowerbirds. Importantly the book dedicates a chapter to Australia's threatened species, which are at risk of extinction due to habitat loss and other environmental pressures. Birds cannot speak for themselves, and it is the hope of the authors that this book will help raise awareness for the ongoing protection and celebration of Australian birds.

ALL IN A FLAP

Many birds have developed powerful wings that give them the ability to fly. They use their wings with exquisite precision and dexterity. Birds need to look after these amazing tools and will fastidiously preen and stretch their wings to keep them in prime condition. This chapter showcases birds using their wings in a variety of ways.

Great Cormorant
Phalacrocorax carbo
LAKE WOLLUMBOOLA, NEW SOUTH WALES

This is the largest of the five cormorant species found in mainland Australia. Cormorants are excellent hunters, catching fish underwater. They have unique feathers which reduce buoyancy, helping them to swim underwater. The downside to these feathers is that they need to be dried out once the bird is out of the water. This is why it is very common to see cormorants resting on the water's edge with their wings splayed wide.

King Penguin

Aptenodytes patagonicus

MACQUARIE ISLAND, TASMANIA

Some birds such as penguins have lost the ability to fly and therefore have very different wings to flying birds. Although they cannot fly in the sky, penguins use their wings extensively to allow them to essentially fly underwater. So their wings are very important in allowing them to catch prey and evade predators. On land penguins also extend their wings for balance and to help control their body temperature in warm conditions.

Jacky Winter
Microeca fascinans
WORRIGEE, NEW SOUTH WALES

Belonging to the Australasian robin family, the Jacky Winter perches on a branch before swooping down to take insects and other bugs on the ground. These birds can be very loyal to certain areas and this one was a regular on an abandoned golf course. The lovely colour in the background is from a reedbed belonging to a disused water feature.

Buller's Albatross
Thalassarche bulleri
WOLLONGONG, NEW SOUTH WALES

A distinctive yellow and black bill combined with a dark face make the adult Buller's Albatross an unmistakably striking bird. The species breeds on several New Zealand offshore islands and is a frequent visitor to Australian waters. There are 22 albatross species worldwide and around 15 species frequent Australian waters on a regular basis. The best way to see an albatross is on a pelagic boat trip. These frequently set out from Australia's major coastal cities – they are usually day trips which take you out to the continental shelf where seabirds are at their most plentiful.

Little Corella
Cacatua sanguinea
NOWRA, NEW SOUTH WALES

One only needs to watch a flock of corellas for a few minutes to recognise that birds do indeed engage in play. These cockatoos can be seen hanging upside down from powerlines, surfing down metal roof tops, wrestling with one another and just having fun. This behaviour and the associated noise of a large flock of corellas must be seen to be believed. It really is a cacophony of the highest order. Their playful nature makes these birds fun to photograph as they are often striking silly poses and using their wings in play.

Red-necked Avocet
Recurvirostra novaehollandiae
LAKE WOLLUMBOOLA, NEW SOUTH WALES

The stunning avocet is one of the our most elegant-looking shorebirds. It is endemic to Australia and one of only four species of avocet in the world. The distinctive upturned bill is used to sift through shallow water in search of prey. They often form large flocks on brackish wetlands, feeding in unison. Shorebirds are always vigilant to the threat of overhead predators such as the Peregrine Falcon. The bird photographed here has heard an alarm call and is running and flapping its wings to take off. Once in flight the birds form large flocks and zigzag across the sky to confuse predators.

Chestnut Teal

Anas castanea

SOUTH NOWRA, NEW SOUTH WALES

A common duck along the east and south-west coasts of Australia. The male is very distinctive with its iridescent green head which is evident in direct sunlight. Ducks will often raise themselves out of the water and flap their wings prior to flying, which was captured above as this bird prepared to depart from a small artificial lake.

Peregrine Falcon
Falco peregrinus
SOUTH COAST, NEW SOUTH WALES

This apex predator among birds uses its incredible speed and large talons to take down prey. Peregrines are masters of flight. They are believed to be the fastest bird in the world during a hunting 'stoop', where they throw their wings back and drop from height in pursuit of prey. This bird was photographed on the NSW coast, where pairs breed on the rocky cliffs. Like most raptors the female (pictured here) is larger than its male counterpart.

Major Mitchell's Cockatoo
Cacatua leadbeateri
CUNNAMULLA, QUEENSLAND

The favourite bird of many and a must-see species for any visiting birder. This uncommon cockatoo inhabits the drier interior of Australia. Like many cockatoos they form large flocks and can often be seen feeding on the ground or ripping open seedpods on trees. They have the most amazing colour in their crest and underwing. Upon landing cockatoos often put on a display, raising their crest and flapping their wings. This is a great moment to capture their stunning colours.

Welcome Swallow
Hirundo neoxena
SOUTH COAST, NEW SOUTH WALES

A species that has mastered the art of flight with its long wings and streamlined body. Swallows are a joy to watch as they move through the air with effortlessness and precision. The Welcome Swallow is common around Australia and is seen in most habitats.

Red-capped Plover
Charadrius ruficapillus
LAKE CONJOLA, NEW SOUTH WALES

A small endemic plover of wetlands and coastal areas all around Australia. The
male is very distinctive with its red cap and is often seen scurrying around chasing
its prey. These birds can be very 'stop start' in their movements, but when prey is
spotted they move very quickly. The bird in the image had been resting on a raised
sand pile and was captured having a wing stretch before moving off.

Little Egret
Egretta garzetta
LAKE WOLLUMBOOLA, NEW SOUTH WALES

A fascinating species to watch as it engages in elaborate acrobatics in its search for a
meal. This egret uses its wings extensively as it dances through the water attempting
to disturb and confuse its prey. The Little Egret can be found in Africa, Europe,
Asia and Australasia. In Australia it favours tidal mudflats, mangroves and fresh and
saltwater wetlands. This bird was part of a group of four individuals that appeared
to be working together as they traversed different areas of the shallow lake.

BREEDING

Birds are absolutely fascinating in all the ways they reproduce. From elaborate bowers to intimate dance and song, birds have filled almost every conceivable niche in the quest to breed. This chapter showcases different species in stages from courtship through to rearing young.

Red-capped Plover
Charadrius ruficapillus
SHOALHAVEN HEADS, NEW SOUTH WALES

The small endemic plover lays its eggs in a shallow scrape on open ground in habitats such as sand bars. The male and female are both involved in the care and parenting of young. When born, the chick has down which blends in with its surroundings in order to hide it from predators. In the image the adult male holds out its wing to protect the newly hatched chick from the wind.

Little Tern
Sternula albifrons
LAKE WOLLUMBOOLA, NEW SOUTH WALES

One of the smallest terns in the world, this species is migratory in its breeding
patterns, traveling down the east coast of Australia in spring from wintering grounds
in northern Australia and Asia. They prefer large open sand bars where they can
form large breeding colonies of more than 100 birds. These colonies are safest
when they have large numbers to help protect the young and fend off intruders.
Unfortunately, the pressures of human interference have drastically reduced suitable
habitat and young birds are prone to predation by dogs, cats, foxes and aerial
predators. This has led to the species being listed as 'Endangered' in Queensland,
New South Wales and Tasmania. Thankfully volunteers all around Australia spend
countless hours setting up fences and guarding the birds from both humans and
predators. The author would like to thank Frances Bray at Lake Wollumboola for
her dedication and perseverance in protecting this species.

Red-browed Finch

Neochmia temporalis

WARBY RANGES, VICTORIA

A common endemic finch along the east coast of Australia. Many finches, including this species, have a variety of displays during courtship. This bird was observed carrying around a grass stem from perch to perch trying to impress the females.

Satin Bowerbird
Ptilonorhynchus violaceus
CALLALA BAY, NEW SOUTH WALES

Among of the most fascinating courtship displays are those of the bowerbird family.
The males usually go to extraordinary lengths to create a bower which is often some
sort of construction of twigs and plant material. The Satin Bowerbird famously
collects anything blue and places it in front of his bower. This can include pegs,
bottle tops and straws. The female will attend the bower on multiple occasions
to inspect the male's work and if she is not happy he will tear it down and start
all over again. Once she is satisfied, he gets the reward of mating with the female.
This behaviour is truly extraordinary.

Beautiful Firetail
Stagonopleura bella
MELALEUCA, TASMANIA

An uncommon bird on the mainland, featuring only in suitable habitat around the south-east of the country. It is more common on Tasmania which still has plenty of suitable habitat for this species to thrive. These birds were photographed in some of the most pristine wilderness Australia has to offer on the West Coast of Tasmania.

Australasian Swamphen
Porphyrio melanotus
ULLADULLA, NEW SOUTH WALES

A very common bird on wetlands around Australia which has adapted well to
artificial lakes. Adults have a distinctive red bill and frontal shield and flick their
tail as they walk. Swamphens breed in sedges and grasses adjacent to wetlands.
The young are black and have large feet with poorly formed wings, giving them an
unusual gangly appearance.

Australian Masked-Owl
Tyto novaehollandiae
TASMANIA

There are five owls in the genus *Tyto* in Australia, with this species being larger, darker and stronger than the Eastern Barn Owl. They require large old trees with hollows to breed and raise their young. This species is somewhat elusive and can be hard to locate, so the author was very happy to photograph an adult and a young bird together.

Red-capped Plover
Charadrius ruficapillus
LAKE WOLLUMBOOLA, NEW SOUTH WALES

The author captured this male Red-capped Plover running with an eggshell. It is likely that the bird is removing the shell from the nest so that aerial predators are not made aware of the chick. This behaviour is not fully understood, however it is common among shorebirds.

41

Great Crested Grebe
Podiceps cristatus
LAKE WALLACE, NEW SOUTH WALES

The largest and arguably the most striking grebe in Australia, these birds are fun to
observe as the young will climb all over the adults, often perching on their backs
while they are small enough.

Royal Penguin
Eudyptes schlegeli
MACQUARIE ISLAND, TASMANIA

Deep in the Southern Ocean, halfway between Australia and Antarctica, lays Macquarie Island. It is a narrow island about 34km in length. This island holds a broad variety of birdlife including a large rookery of Royal Penguins. The adults share parenting duty with one penguin guarding the chick while the other is out fishing. What is incredible to watch is how a returning penguin can locate its partner and chick among the cacophony of noise and thousands of other birds.

Black Swan
Cygnus atratus
PYREE, NEW SOUTH WALES

The Black Swan is the essence of elegance. It is so graceful when moving through
the water and is a very attractive bird. Black Swans are mostly monogamous, pairing
for life. What is not well known is that around 25 per cent of pairs are homosexual
males. They form a bond with a female and once she lays the eggs they drive her
from the nest, incubating and raising the chicks themselves. Once the young fledge,
the adults form very large flocks and go through a large moult which renders them
flightless until their new feathers grow.

BUSHLAND

Australia's national anthem says it best with:
"Our land abounds in nature's gifts, of beauty rich
and rare." This is no exaggeration, with a myriad of
habitat types including rainforests, woodlands, coastal
heath and alpine mountains to name just a few.

Birds have filled every niche in every habitat,
making the most of the opportunities on offer.
This chapter showcases the diverse array of birds that
inhabit the bush.

Pink Robin
Petroica rodinogaster
OTWAY RANGES, VICTORIA

A bird so beautiful that people struggle to believe it is real. The colour is so striking
one wonders how and why it evolved to be this way. No doubt it has something to
do with impressing females and standing out. The Pink Robin is not commonly
seen as it prefers the dark, wet rainforests of Tasmania and southern Victoria.

Laughing Kookaburra
Dacelo novaeguineae
DENILIQUIN, NEW SOUTH WALES

Possibly Australia's most iconic species. Well known for its incredible laughing
song, which is often heard in the morning. If a few birds join the chorus it becomes
quite a racket. Common in forests along the east coast and in southern Australia.
The species has been introduced to Tasmania and southern Western Australia. It
can adapt well to human activity and is often reasonably tame in inhabited areas.

Glossy Black-Cockatoo
Calyptorhynchus lathami
SOUTHERN HIGHLANDS, NEW SOUTH WALES

The smallest of the five black-cockatoo species found in Australia. Occurs mainly on the east coast where suitable habitat remains. Evolved to feed strictly on casuarinas (sheoak), but unfortunately these trees have been heavily cleared since European settlement, resulting in the birds having limited food available. Listed as Threatened in New South Wales.

Red-capped Robin
Petroica goodenovii
WARBY RANGES, VICTORIA

This diminutive robin of inland Australia is appropriately named. It is relatively common in open woodlands with grassy areas. The birds can often be seen sitting on open branches, watching the ground for any type of movement that could indicate prey.

Overleaf: The male has a bright red breast and crown while the female is dull greyish-brown with a small amount of red on the crown. The pair often feed together and can often be heard calling to one another.

Spotted Pardalote

Pardalotus punctatus

CALLALA BAY, NEW SOUTH WALES

One of four pardalote species found in Australia and arguably the prettiest. With a very loud repetitive call this dazzling bird is often heard before it is seen. It occurs in a wide variety of eucalypt forests around eastern, southern and south-western Australia. The bird in the image can be identified as a male due to the bright yellow chest and dark cap with white spots.

Powerful Owl

Ninox strenua

CALLALA BAY, NEW SOUTH WALES

The largest owl in Australia preys on mammals and birds and requires a large territory. It generally inhabits extensive areas of mostly wet coastal forests which support good populations of prey species and contain large tree hollows in which they can nest. Its distribution extends along the east coast of Australia to south-east Australia. Due to habitat loss and other pressures it is listed as Vulnerable in New South Wales.

Australian Magpie
Gymnorhina tibicen
CANBERRA, AUSTRALIAN CAPITAL TERRITORY

The iconic magpie is one of the most recognised birds in Australia. Its beautiful song is synonymous with the Australian landscape and is a welcome sound anywhere you go. Magpies are found in all types of habitat around Australia and it is unusual not to see this bird whilst traveling. The species was named after the Eurasian Magpie by early settlers but is not related to that bird; it is most closely related to the butcherbirds.

Diamond Dove

Geopelia cuneata

NORTHERN TERRITORY

A tiny dove that travels the dry interior of Australia in pursuit of suitable habitat. It prefers grassy woodland with a source of water nearby, feeding on fallen seeds. After good rain produces plentiful food they can breed in large numbers, with the increased population dispersing far and wide. The beautiful bright red eye and orbital skin is very distinctive, allowing for easy identification.

Grey-crowned Babbler
Pomatostomus temporalis
GOONDAWINDI, QUEENSLAND

Babblers are a wonderful family of birds and a favourite among many birdwatchers. They are communal birds, feeding and traveling as a group, and are also unique in that all members of the group help to raise the young – no doubt a strategy that ensures the greatest survival of young in sometimes harsh outback conditions. Grey-crowned Babblers prefer open woodland in central and northern Australia. When encountered the constant chatter among members of the group is very noticeable. They are great fun to watch as they go from tree to tree looking for food.

Gang-gang Cockatoo
Callocephalon fimbriatum
LITHGOW, NEW SOUTH WALES

A stunningly beautiful and charismatic species. The male has the red head and crest while the female is dark grey with a hint of red and yellow on the breast and belly. Gang-gangs are typically found in higher-altitude habitat in alpine-type areas. However, they do also frequent more coastal temperate forests, especially in autumn and winter. They have a very distinctive call which is often likened to the noise made by a squeaky barn door.

Hooded Robin
Melanodryas cucullata
CUNNAMULLA, QUEENSLAND

An open woodland specialist, the Hooded Robin prefers open areas with plenty of
deadfall and perches to feed from. It is one of the largest robins in Australia with
the male having the distinctive black hood, while the female is a uniform pale grey.
They are almost always seen in pairs.

Pale-yellow Robin

Tregellasia capito

FAR NORTH QUEENSLAND

A small large-headed robin that is a rainforest specialist. It has two distinct populations: one in far north Queensland which has buff lores illustrated here; the second in northern New South Wales and southern Queensland. It also has very distinctive yellow legs which separate it from the similar Eastern Yellow Robin.

Southern Boobook
Ninox boobook
SOUTH COAST, NEW SOUTH WALES

A relatively common owl which occurs throughout Australia wherever large trees
exist for it to roost and breed. It has a very distinctive onomatopoeic call and is
often heard calling constantly. There are four recognised subspecies in Australia
which exhibit variations in plumage.

FEEDING

The large variety of both flora and fauna in Australia has led to numerous food sources for birds. Through the beauty of evolution, birds have evolved to exploit nearly every possible niche. From nectar to rabbits and insects to reptiles, birds target them all.

This chapter features birds feeding on many different food types.

Black Kite
Milvus migrans
WESTERN QUEENSLAND

A sad sight on many Australian roads is the large number of native animals killed by vehicles. Due to roadkill there is an abundance of food for carrion feeders such as kites, eagles and ravens. Black Kites are very common on inland roads where the amount of roadkill is high. Thankfully these birds appear to have very good road sense, rarely being hit themselves by oncoming vehicles.

Eastern Spinebill
Acanthorhynchus tenuirostris
WEST NOWRA, NEW SOUTH WALES

A small honeyeater that is common along the coast from Queensland to South
Australia and including Tasmania. It is a frequent visitor to backyards and gardens
which have native plants such as Grevillea and Callistemon. The spinebill is a
nectar-feeding specialist, with its long decurved bill perfect for getting deep into
flowers. Spinebills will often hover when feeding in order to reach the best flowers.
They are often chased by larger dominant honeyeaters such as wattlebirds.

Major Mitchell's Cockatoo
Cacatua leadbeateri
WESTERN QUEENSLAND

A striking cockatoo of the dry interior which is often called the Pink Cockatoo.
This bird can be seen travelling in flocks over large distances in search of food.
They commonly feed on the ground, eating seeds and other fallen plant matter.
Like many cockatoos, they have a very strong bill allowing them to crack open seed
pods to access seeds within.

Black-shouldered Kite
Elanus axillaris
LAKE WOLLUMBOOLA, NEW SOUTH WALES
A supreme hunter of small rodents, this bird hovers in the sky scanning
the ground for movement and then swooping down on prey.

Grey Plover
Pluvialis squatarola
LAKE WOLLUMBOOLA, NEW SOUTH WALES

One of many migratory waders that fly all the way from the Northern Hemisphere to Australia. These birds spend the Australian summer fattening up, feeding on sandworms and other invertebrates found on tidal flats. Different wader species have different bill lengths, allowing them to target a wider variety of prey hiding in the mud.

Superb Fairy-wren
Malurus cyaneus
WARBY RANGES, VICTORIA

This fairy-wren is a prolific hunter of invertebrates, including small insects and worms. Fairy-wrens form small feeding territories in which they hunt predominantly by hopping on the ground looking for tasty morsels hiding under rocks and in shrubs. The male photographed here was collecting prey before delivering it to a nest with young.

White-bellied Sea-Eagle

Haliaeetus leucogaster

CALLALA BAY, NEW SOUTH WALES

An impressive eagle that is second in size only to the Wedge-tailed Eagle among
Australian raptors. This large bird inhabits coastal areas and large inland wetlands
where it predominantly hunts fish using its large talons to catch them and
then its powerful wings to carry its prey to a nearby tree. The juvenile sea-eagle
has completely different plumage to the adult, being mottled brown and easily
confusable with a Wedge-tailed Eagle.

Beach Stone-curlew

Esacus magnirostris

ORIENT POINT, NEW SOUTH WALES

This uncommon large wader inhabits coastal areas and tidal mangroves.
It prefers quiet areas away from humans and loves to feed on blue soldier crabs
(*Mictyris longicarpus*) which are often abundant. This bird gorged itself on small
crabs until it could eat no more.

Great Crested Grebe
Podiceps cristatus
LAKE WALLACE, NEW SOUTH WALES

These beautiful grebes are very diligent parents, caring for multiple chicks.
The adults bring a non-stop supply of small fish which the chicks grab with
their pincer-like bills. When small the chicks often lay on the back of a parent,
as captured opposite, having their dinner delivered straight to them.

Yellow-billed Spoonbill
Platalea flavipes
GOONDIWINDI, QUEENSLAND

One of two spoonbill species that inhabit Australia, the other being the Royal Spoonbill which has a black bill. This bird uses its remarkably shaped bill to filter through mud in shallow water. Once it detects prey, it closes its bill and captures a meal. This bird was very effective at catching small yabbies in an inland waterway.

Mulga Parrot
Psephotus varius
GLUEPOT RESERVE, SOUTH AUSTRALIA

Many birds are monogamous, forming lifelong pair bonds. Mulga Parrots are one such species, with the male and female preferring each other's company to that of a larger flock. To reaffirm and strengthen that bond one bird will feed the other. This image – taken in late winter before spring breeding – captured the male feeding his partner.

Yellow-tailed Black-Cockatoo
Calyptorhynchus funereus
CULBURRA BEACH, NEW SOUTH WALES

This stunning and very large cockatoo has distinctive yellow patches on the ear-coverts
and tail. They are often heard and seen on Coastal Banksias up and down the coast
from Queensland to South Australia. They use their very strong bills to rip open the
seed pods from this tree, as pictured here.

Gang-gang Cockatoo
Callocephalon fimbriatum
LITHGOW, NEW SOUTH WALES

The simply breathtaking Gang-gang Cockatoo has taken a liking to the introduced hawthorn shrub (*Crataegus monogyna*). This weed spreads rapidly, no doubt in part due to the Gang-gang's love of the seeds found in the small red berries the plant produces. Most years the Gang-gangs come down from the eucalypts and flock to areas which have large growths of hawthorn shrubs.

FLIGHT

To see a bird fly is to witness the magic of evolution. Once birds gained the ability to fly, they were able to colonise the globe and reach prey that was once off-limits. This chapter showcases birds doing what they do best – flying.

White-bellied Sea-Eagle
Haliaeetus leucogaster
CALLALA BAY, NEW SOUTH WALES

One of two large raptors in Australia which feed predominantly on fish, the other being the Eastern Osprey. This impressive bird is easily observed gliding through the air above the coast and large water bodies. Its very large wings and tail feathers enable it to fly with large prey in its talons.

Short-tailed Shearwater
Ardenna tenuirostris
EAGLEHAWK NECK, TASMANIA

Each year Short-tailed Shearwaters undertake a massive return migration from their
breeding grounds in Australia and Tasmania all the way to the North Pacific, often

north of the Arctic Circle. It is believed that they cover up to 15,000km on their
journey. Upon their return huge flocks can be seen along the coast of Australia.
The author was lucky to witness such an event off Tasmania as thousands of
birds flew south.

Peregrine Falcon
Falco peregrinus
SOUTH COAST, NEW SOUTH WALES

Believed to be the fastest bird in the world, the Peregrine uses extreme speed to catch its prey unaware as it drops from the sky. Its large talons and speed combined often kill prey upon impact. The falcon has evolved special baffles in its nostrils to allow it to breathe when travelling at such great speeds.

Bar-breasted Honeyeater

Ramsayornis fasciatus

FOGG DAM, NORTHERN TERRITORY

A honeyeater of far north Australia which prefers swampy type habitat where it feeds on nectar and insects. Many honeyeaters can hover while flying, allowing them to hawk for insects as seen here.

Wandering Albatross
Diomedea exulans
WOLLONGONG, NEW SOUTH WALES

The largest bird to visit Australian shores is the master of the sea. The biggest individuals can have a wingspan of 3.5m. These seabirds are truly magnificent

to watch and photos just cannot do justice to their size and the grace with which they fly. The bird pictured here – with smaller Short-tailed Shearwaters (*Ardenna tenuirostris*) – is the New Zealand form of Wandering Albatross, which is sometimes 'split' as a separate species, Gibson's Albatross (*Diomedea gibsoni*). It breeds on New Zealand Subantarctic Islands.

Black-browed Albatross
Thalassarche melanophris
WOLLONGONG, NEW SOUTH WALES

Many people may be surprised to learn that are more than 20 recognised species
of albatross in the world, with the majority of these frequenting Australian waters.
One such species is the Black-browed Albatross. Although much smaller than
the Wandering Albatross it is still a large bird with a wingspan of up to 2.4m.
Surprisingly these birds can live for up to 70 years and they spend their entire lives
at sea except when they come to land to breed. They truly are exceptional masters of
flight and glide with ease over the expansive ocean.

Pied Oystercatcher
Haematopus longirostris
SHOALHAVEN HEADS, NEW SOUTH WALES

These shorebirds spend the majority of their time walking large intertidal mudflats looking for prey. The bird opposite had been chased off by another pair who were not happy with its presence. Amazingly, in the image above a clam has fought back by clamping itself onto the toe of the oystercatcher, causing the bird to hop around on one foot and call out in distress.

White-winged Black Tern
Chlidonias leucopterus
LAKE WOLLUMBOOLA, NEW SOUTH WALES

The name of this species can be confusing in Australia as it is most frequently seen in non-breeding plumage as shown here. It is not until late April or May that the birds start to develop their breeding plumage with a black body and white wings. This tern is found in freshwater and saline wetlands from inland to the coast. It has a distinctive low looping flight style as it searches for prey.

Welcome Swallow
Hirundo neoxena
SHOALHAVEN HEADS, NEW SOUTH WALES

Swallows were designed with flight in mind. Their long wings and slender profile give them unparalleled skill in the sky. In certain areas populations are large and landing space is at a premium. The birds photographed above were having quite a disagreement.

Black-browed Albatross
Thalassarche melanophris
WOLLONGONG, NEW SOUTH WALES

It is amazing to see how birds have evolved to become masters of flight.

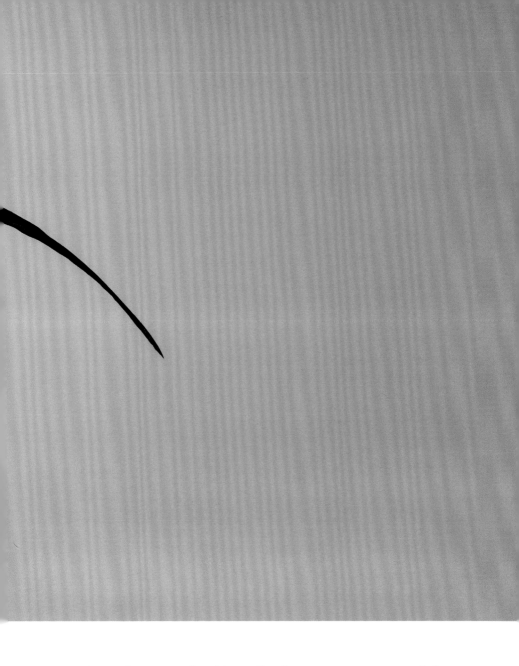

They use their wings, tails and feet to allow them to manoeuvre in a myriad of ways.
This image shows how the albatross uses its feet and tail-feathers to slow down
and steady itself for landing. It is no surprise that aircraft use many of the same
techniques as birds when flying.

GRASSLANDS

Australia is home to extensive native grasslands which support a wide range of flora and fauna.

More recently, as humans have cleared swathes of forest for agriculture, some birds have adapted to this now pervasive habitat. This chapter showcases the birds that live in native and exotic grasslands.

Emu
Dromaius novaehollandiae
HAY PLAINS, NEW SOUTH WALES

An iconic species that adorns Australia's coat of arms, the Emu roams over large areas of grassland grazing on small shrubs, grasses and insects. It is Australia's largest bird and is mainly found inland away from large cities.

Chestnut Quail-thrush

Cinclosoma castanotum

HATTAH, VICTORIA

A Mallee specialist that lives in areas with spinifex and other native grasses and shrubs. This bird is ground dwelling and often skulks in the undergrowth. They are usually seen in pairs and can be quite trusting of humans.

Singing Honeyeater
Lichenostomus virescens
SWAN HILL, VICTORIA

A common honeyeater across most of Australia which is well adapted to living in grasslands with small shrubs. Feeds on nectar, insects and small berries and has a distinctive call which is a common sound in most grasslands.

Double-barred Finch
Taeniopygia bichenovii
CAPERTEE VALLEY, NEW SOUTH WALES
A very small finch found in the far north of Australia and all down the east coast.
It prefers open grasslands and can often be seen perched on fences along roadways.

Brolga

Grus rubicunda

WESTERN QUEENSLAND

A very large bird that inhabits a range of habitats, usually close to water.
Brolgas are often seen on open fields and grasslands where they feed on both
plant and animal matter.

Nankeen Kestrel
Falco cenchroides
SOUTH COAST, NEW SOUTH WALES

One of Australia's smallest raptors, this kestrel is well suited to grassland habitat.
It hunts a wide variety of prey allowing it to make the most of whatever food source
is abundant. It feeds on small mammals, reptiles, birds and insects. It often hunts
from rocks or by hovering in the sky and dropping down onto prey.

Red-tailed Black-Cockatoo
Calyptorhynchus banksii
WESTERN QUEENSLAND

The most widespread of the black-cockatoos with populations found in a range of
habitats including extensive grasslands in western Queensland. Often feeds on seeds
on the ground and can form large feeding flocks when conditions are suitable.

Tasmanian Native-hen
Tribonyx mortierii
SOUTH-EAST TASMANIA

The endemic Tasmanian Native-hen is only found on its eponymous island, where
it replaces the Black-tailed Native-hen of mainland Australia. It inhabits grasslands
and wetlands, where it feeds on grasses and seeds.

Cape Barren Goose
Cereopsis novaehollandiae
BRUNY ISLAND, TASMANIA

A large grey goose that inhabits coastal areas of southern Australia and Tasmania.
They feed on native grasses but have adapted well to sown pasture. They rarely swim
and prefer to walk away from potential danger prior to flying.

PORTRAITS

Few people get to see the beauty of birds first hand. This chapter shows birds in all their glory up close and personal. The uniqueness of shape, size and colour is even more evident when viewed in detail.

Red-capped Robin
Petroica goodenovii
WARBY RANGES, VICTORIA

The stunningly beautiful Red-capped Robin is a highlight of any inland trip. They prefer open woodland habitat with plenty of deadfall and branches to perch on. The male has the bright red cap and breast which make him really stand out.

Great Cormorant
Phalacrocorax carbo
LAKE WOLLUMBOOLA, NEW SOUTH WALES

The largest cormorant species in Australia. This individual has very intense blue
colouring around the eye, which is not common in this species and indicates that it
is in peak breeding condition.

Pied Cormorant
Phalacrocorax varius
SOUTH COAST, NEW SOUTH WALES

Another large cormorant. Its distinctive black-and-white plumage separates it from
the slightly larger Great Cormorant. You don't get to fully appreciate the wonderful
colour around the eye until you see the bird up close.

Double-banded Plover
Charadrius bicinctus
LAKE CONJOLA, NEW SOUTH WALES

A true ANZAC bird and the only Australian wader to migrate east-west to New Zealand. The birds that arrive in Australia in February come from the South Island of New Zealand. They spend the winter in Australia before moulting into their distinctive reddish double-banded breeding plumage as shown here. They then migrate back to New Zealand to breed during spring.

Nankeen Kestrel
Falco cenchroides
SOUTH COAST, NEW SOUTH WALES

It really is amazing to see birds up close where you get to admire their plumage and physical features. The kestrel is no exception with its lovely rufous feathers and its hook-tipped bill that enables it to tear apart prey. The female shown here has an all rufous head.

Eastern Barn Owl
Tyto delicatula
SOUTH COAST, NEW SOUTH WALES

Barn owls are among the most widespread and best-known owl species throughout
the world. Australia is fortunate to have five species in the barn owl family with the
Eastern Barn Owl being the most common. They have a very distinctive facial disk
and pale plumage in Australia, distinguishing them from other similar owls.

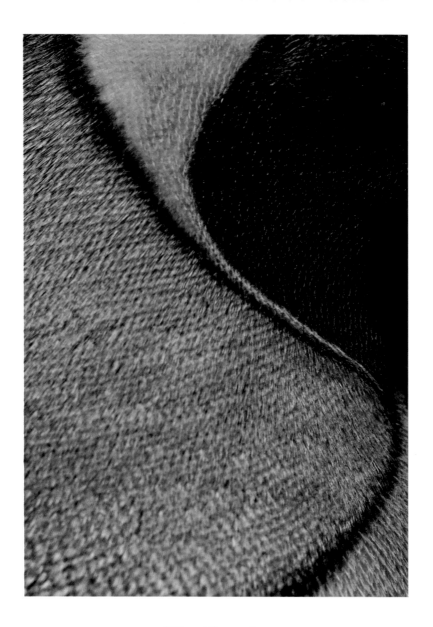

King Penguin
Aptenodytes patagonicus
MACQUARIE ISLAND, TASMANIA

A unique and striking penguin that inhabits the Subantarctic islands to the south
of Australia. A close-up portrait illustrates the incredible colour and patterns found
in this species.

Gang-gang Cockatoo
Callocephalon fimbriatum
LITHGOW, NEW SOUTH WALES

This is one of the most charismatic birds in Australia. The male has a
red head with the forward-curling crest which is unique to this species.
The juvenile male shown here is just starting to develop its adult male
plumage with the red feathers coming through.

Beach Stone-curlew
Esacus magnirostris
ORIENT POINT, NEW SOUTH WALES

An interesting-looking shorebird with its big head, large bill and bright yellow
eye. This stone-curlew uses its large bill to catch crabs and other small marine
invertebrates in tidal mudflats and coastal areas.

Australian King-Parrot
Alisterus scapularis
BANGALEE, NEW SOUTH WALES

A large parrot which is a frequent visitor to bird feeders up and down the east coast of Australia. This bird becomes very tame, often eating sunflower seeds from a person's hand. The adult male is predominantly red while the female is green. Young males are green before they start moulting into their adult plumage, as shown here.

Crested Pigeon
Ocyphaps lophotes
BEECHWORTH, VICTORIA

One of the coolest-looking pigeons in Australia is the aptly named Crested Pigeon. This species has a very large crest that extends well past its head, giving it a unique appearance. The Crested Pigeon is very widespread around Australia and has become a lot more common in recent years in the east. It is now a frequent visitor to many parks and open grasslands where it can be seen feeding on the ground.

Tasmanian Native-hen
Tribonyx mortierii
SOUTH-EAST TASMANIA

This Tasmanian endemic is a lot more confiding than its mainland counterpart the
Black-tailed Native-hen, allowing this detailed portrait. The heavy bill in this species
is well suited to ripping up grass roots and cutting vegetation before eating.

Little Tern
Sternula albifrons
LAKE WOLLUMBOOLA, NEW SOUTH WALES

The Little Tern is a real battler. It migrates thousands of kilometres each year and once it finds a suitable nest site on a sand bar it then has to protect its eggs and chicks from numerous predators. Once the chick hatches, both parents hunt almost non-stop in order to bring back small fish. When a chick hears a parent returning it starts calling vociferously until it is fed. The adults use their aerobatic skills to perfection, often dropping off the fish without landing before leaving to find more food.

Satin Bowerbird

Ptilonorhynchus violaceus

BANGALEE, NEW SOUTH WALES

One of the better-known bowerbirds, this species is a common visitor to many gardens on the east coast of Australia. The females and young males have green plumage and it is only after five years that the males begin to attain their satin blue feathers. The purple eye is distinctive and spectacular.

Red-tailed Black-Cockatoo

Calyptorhynchus banksii

QUEENSLAND

Black-cockatoos are simply stunning birds and the plumage of this species is remarkable. This detailed portrait beautifully illustrates the small yellow spots that can be hard to see at a distance.

THE GARDEN

Backyards play a very important role in providing shelter, food and water for native birds. By creating a bird-friendly garden with native plants you will be helping your local birds by providing somewhere for them to eat, sleep and play. This chapter showcases some of the many birds that visit gardens around Australia.

Eastern Spinebill
Acanthorhynchus tenuirostris
BANGALEE, NEW SOUTH WALES

A very active and fast-moving honeyeater which is often seen in gardens up and down the east coast of Australia. This species has evolved to have a bill that is the ultimate tool for reaching into flowers and acquiring the sweet nectar contained within. The small size of this honeyeater often results in it being chased and bullied by the larger wattlebirds and miners. It is a good idea to include plants with small flowers which the spinebill can reach but the large birds cannot.

Common Bronzewing

Phaps chalcoptera

CALLALA BAY, NEW SOUTH WALES

A bird that is found all around Australia in a wide variety of habitats. It is much more common in areas surrounded by national parks or large areas of woodland. While these birds are wary in the bush they can become tame in backyards and are regular visitors to water bowls and bird feeders. They have distinct booming calls and can be seen loafing around under trees.

Eastern Yellow Robin
Eopsaltria australis
BANGALEE, NEW SOUTH WALES

A reasonably common robin on the east coast of Australia which can be seen
clinging to the trunks of trees or perched on branches as shown here. They are very
trusting of humans and will quickly become gardening companions if a tasty worm
is on offer. The male and female both have a yellow breast and grey head.

Satin Bowerbird
Ptilonorhynchus violaceus
CENTRAL COAST, NEW SOUTH WALES

The beautiful but destructive Satin Bowerbird is a common garden visitor along
the east coast. The adult male, pictured here, is less common than the young males

and females which are green. The male can take six to seven years to develop the satin blue plumage. Some people may be lucky enough to have an active bower in their yard, where the male impresses the female with his bower-building and decorating skills.

Willie Wagtail
Rhipidura leucophrys
WEST NOWRA, NEW SOUTH WALES

A common and much loved visitor to nearly every garden in Australia. This bird can be seen in nearly every habitat, often perched on a fence or flying from rock to rock, wagging its tail and calling out.

Scarlet Honeyeater
Myzomela sanguinolenta
CALLALA BAY, NEW SOUTH WALES

This diminutive and stunning honeyeater is found on the east coast of Australia
and is often seen feeding on flowering Callistemon and Banksia. The red-and-black
plumage of the adult male makes it a striking sight in any garden.

Musk Lorikeet
Glossopsitta concinna
NOWRA, NEW SOUTH WALES

Australia is home to hundreds of different eucalypt trees which have an array of flowers. Many Australian birds, including the Musk Lorikeet, have evolved to feed on the nectar the flowers provide. In exchange for a meal the birds pollinate the plants as they go from tree to tree feeding.

Red Wattlebird
Anthochaera carunculata
LAKE BOGA, VICTORIA

A large common honeyeater found in the southern half of Australia.
The prominent red wattles on the side of the head aid identification. Can be
very aggressive towards other birds when defending flowering plants. Honeyeaters
along with lorikeets are the two main families of birds that feed on the nectar
produced by eucalypts and many other flowering plants. The dominant flower
colour is red, however many other colours also exist, including the yellow on this
profusely flowering eucalypt.

Grey Shrike-thrush
Colluricincla harmonica
BANGALEE, NEW SOUTH WALES

This bird, which has arguably the most beautiful song of any species in the bush, is common in gardens all around Australia where there are enough trees for it to feed and sing.

Australian King-Parrot
Alisterus scapularis
BANGALEE, NEW SOUTH WALES

The large but very friendly king-parrot is a welcome visitor to many gardens. It loves sunflower seeds and will quickly eat from a person's hand if fed on a regular basis. The male has a red body and green wings, while the female has a green head and red belly.

Superb Fairy-wren
Malurus cyaneus
CALALLA BAY, NEW SOUTH WALES

The much loved and admired Superb Fairy-wren is a highlight in any garden.
This species prefers locations with small dense shrubs to provide cover and open
areas to feed. The male's beautiful blue cap, cheeks and back make it stand out
from other birds in the garden.

New Holland Honeyeater

Phylidonyris novaehollandiae

SOUTH NOWRA, NEW SOUTH WALES

A common and distinctive honeyeater found in south-west and south-east Australia including Tasmania. This species actively feeds on flowering plants such as Callistemon and Grevillea. They will often become aggressive towards other birds to protect the valued nectar.

Laughing Kookaburra
Dacelo novaeguineae
CALLALA BAY, NEW SOUTH WALES

A common garden visitor that is often observed perched on a branch looking for
prey such as small reptiles. The kookaburra is often one of the first birds heard in
the morning, giving its unmistakable raucous calls. It also has the distinction of
being the world's largest kingfisher species.

Rose Robin
Petroica rosea
CALLALA BAY, NEW SOUTH WALES

Some gardens on the east coast will be lucky enough to be visited by the beautiful Rose Robin. This tiny robin often feeds at the top of eucalypts but will sometimes come down for a drink. The bird has a lovely call that once heard will not be forgotten.

THE COAST

Australia's coastline stretches for more than 25,000km, providing prime habitat for numerous bird species. These birds have evolved to take advantage of the bountiful resources the ocean and coastal areas provide. This chapter highlights the birds that live in this rugged and often challenging environment.

Great Egret
Ardea alba
LAKE WOLLUMBOOLA, NEW SOUTH WALES

The largest egret species in Australia has an extremely long neck which it uses extensively when feeding. It is a reasonably common sight on the coast and can often be seen standing in the shallows hunting for prey.

Hooded Plover
Thinornis cucullatus
BRUNY ISLAND, TASMANIA

This small endemic shorebird is striking with its black head and red eye-ring. The Hooded Plover was once common around the southern coastline of Australia and Tasmania. However, with human disturbance and introduced predators, this beach-nesting bird has suffered a serious decline in numbers. Fortunately, there is a large volunteer network working tirelessly to protect and assist this vulnerable species.

Red-capped Plover
Charadrius ruficapillus
LAKE WOLLUMBOOLA, NEW SOUTH WALES

A species that is reasonably common, but due to its very small size and habit of
fleeing from humans it can be hard to sight. Red-capped Plovers favour large sand
bars and tidal mudflats and are often seen standing in the shallows looking for prey.
The adult male (pictured) is distinguished from females and immatures by its red cap.

Curlew Sandpiper

Calidris ferruginea

LAKE WOLLUMBOOLA, NEW SOUTH WALES (LEFT)

WERRIBEE TREATMENT PLANT, VICTORIA (ABOVE)

In non-breeding plumage this is a plain-looking migratory shorebird that can often
be mistaken for various other species. The best identification feature is its decurved
bill, which it uses like a sewing machine as it prods the mud looking for prey. In
March and April the drab grey-brown feathers are replaced by striking chestnut
breeding plumage.

Bar-tailed Godwit
Limosa lapponica
LAKE WOLLUMBOOLA, NEW SOUTH WALES

A large migratory shorebird which arrives in Australia in its pale brownish non-breeding plumage. This incredible bird holds the record for the longest non-stop flight of 11,000km from Alaska to New Zealand. Australia is lucky to have birds from both Alaska and Siberia visit its shores each year. Like most shorebirds, before they migrate north to breed, they moult into their striking rufous breeding plumage.

Red-capped Plover
Charadrius ruficapillus
LAKE WOLLUMBOOLA, NEW SOUTH WALES

Many birds choose to nest and raise their young on the coast. One such species is the Red-capped Plover, which lays its eggs in a scrape in the sand. Once the chick hatches it almost immediately starts following the adults and feeding itself. Unfortunately, due to human disturbance and introduced predators, these birds face an uphill battle to reach adulthood.

Red-necked Stint
Calidris ruficollis
SHOALHAVEN HEADS, NEW SOUTH WALES

The smallest migratory wader to regularly visit Australia's coastline each year.
This tiny shorebird weighs as little as 28g when it arrives from its breeding grounds
in Siberia. The Red-necked Stint spends the summer in Australia moulting and
feeding until it leaves in early April weighing more than 40 per cent more than
it did upon arrival. This fuel allows it to make the arduous journey back to the
Northern Hemisphere. This is reason enough to ensure Australia's tidal mudflats
and coastlines are being protected to provide enough food for these migratory birds.

Silver Gull
Chroicocephalus novaehollandiae
ULLADULLA, NEW SOUTH WALES

This species is the most widespread and common gull in Australia and its population has increased dramatically in numbers due to its exploitation of food sources from humans. Silver Gulls are found around the entire coastline of Australia and it is very rare to be by the sea and not see them. The bird photographed here is in adult plumage with the red legs and bill.

Double-banded Plover
Charadrius bicinctus
SHOALHAVEN HEADS, NEW SOUTH WALES

Sunrise and sunset along the coast of Australia is a wonderful time to observe birds.
They are often very active feeding at these times as the sun casts a warm glow over
the surroundings.

Pacific Golden Plover
Pluvialis fulva
SHOALHAVEN HEADS, NEW SOUTH WALES

One of several species of migratory shorebirds that visit Australia during the austral summer. The Pacific Golden Plover is unique with its golden plumage, easily separating it from other shorebirds. This species undergoes a drastic plumage change from a uniform pale yellowish to the impressive breeding plumage shown opposite. It is an uncommon coastal specialist which is at home on both tidal mudflats and rocky outcrops. Like many shorebirds it can be difficult to approach, which makes viewing a challenge.

Kelp Gull

Larus dominicanus

SOUTH-EAST TASMANIA

Australia has some very impressive sheer rock cliffs on its coastline, which have
plentiful ledges that gulls and other birds often rest upon. The Kelp Gull pictured
here is a lot larger than the more common Silver Gull.

Sharp-tailed Sandpiper
Calidris acuminata
LAKE WOLLUMBOOLA, NEW SOUTH WALES

One of the more common migratory shorebirds. It favours shallow tidal mudflats around the coast of Australia and can often occur in the hundreds if conditions are favourable. When feeding they will squabble with other birds if they get too close.

THREATENED
SPECIES

Australia has a possible extinction crisis with 134 species of birds listed as 'Threatened' by BirdLife International, comprising 17 classified as 'Critically Endangered', 54 'Endangered' and 63 'Vulnerable'. Australia has already lost 22 bird species to extinction and unless drastic action is taken more are likely to be added to this total.

This chapter showcases some of the birds that are currently listed as threatened species.

Eastern Bristlebird
Dasyornis brachypterus
JERVIS BAY, NEW SOUTH WALES

An 'Endangered' endemic species that is restricted to a few sites along the east coast of Australia. It prefers dense coastal heath-type habitat where it spends most of the time on the ground. It has a beautiful call that it often uses in territorial disputes with other birds. Due to its ground-dwelling behaviour it is prone to attack by cats and foxes. It has also suffered from extensive habitat destruction along the coast for human habitation.

Curlew Sandpiper
Calidris ferruginea
LAKE WOLLUMBOOLA, NEW SOUTH WALES

The Curlew Sandpiper is yet another declining migratory shorebird – classified as 'Near Threatened' – that breeds in the Northern Hemisphere and visits Australia during spring and summer. This species has a strongly decurved bill which helps to separate it from most other small shorebirds. Like all migratory shorebirds, the loss of suitable habitat on its migration route has led to a dramatic decline in numbers. If humans continue to develop and destroy their feeding grounds, extinction is the likely outcome for many shorebird species.

Plains-wanderer
Pedionomus torquatus
DENILIQUIN, NEW SOUTH WALES

One of the world's most unique bird species is endemic to Australia and currently listed as 'Critically Endangered'. This cryptic bird is in a family of its own – the Pedionomidae – with no close living relatives. This Plains-wanderer has suffered from human activities such as habitat destruction and the introduction of non-native predators including foxes and cats. The birds tend to run in an attempt to escape predators instead of flying, leading to their easy capture. They are nomadic in their search for food and can be very difficult to find, making research and monitoring difficult. Their last remaining habitat is the grass plains in the far north of Victoria, through New South Wales and into South Australia.

Forty-spotted Pardalote
Pardalotus quadragintus

BRUNY ISLAND, TASMANIA

An 'Endangered' endemic pardalote of Tasmania that has recently suffered a serious decline in numbers. The major threats are habitat destruction, degradation, and the introduced Sugar Glider. The Difficult Bird Research Group, which has been researching this species, discovered that screw-worm fly larvae are a major cause of mortality in chicks. The fly lays its eggs in the nest and the larvae then burrow into the chick and feed on its flesh, causing high rates of mortality.

Red Knot
Calidris canutus
LAKE WOLLUMBOOLA, NEW SOUTH WALES

The Red Knot is a migratory wader that breeds in the Northern Hemisphere and spends the austral summer in Australia. They use the East Asian-Australasian Flyway to migrate between Australia and their breeding grounds in Russia and Alaska. This species suffered catastrophic losses when the South Korean government built the Saemangeum sea wall. This wall prevented water from reaching 400 sq km of tidal mudflats which supported up to 400,000 shorebirds including thousands of Red Knots. Unfortunately, most of the shorebirds that relied on this site were probably unable to find sufficient food elsewhere and most likely perished. The species is currently classified as 'Near Threatened'.

Shy Albatross
Thalassarche cauta
EAGLEHAWK NECK, TASMANIA

Australia is fortunate enough to have the Shy Albatross as an endemic breeder on three islands around Tasmania: Albatross, Pedra Branca and Mewstone Islands. With a population of around 25,000 birds and only three breeding locations, the species is susceptible to disease or a natural disaster which could severely reduce its numbers. It is listed as 'Near Threatened'. One of the main threats to the survival of albatrosses is longline fishing, because the birds eat the bait and are often caught on the hooks and subsequently drown.

Mallee Emu-wren

Stipiturus mallee

HATTAH-KULKYNE NATIONAL PARK, VICTORIA

The tiny Mallee Emu-wren has evolved to survive in very thick spinifex grass in the Mallee areas of north-west Victoria and South Australia. Sadly, Mallee habitat was deemed to be of no value and an enormous amount of it was cleared for agriculture. As its habitat shrunk, this bird's vulnerability to wildfires increased and with each fire it lost more and more habitat. At present the Mallee Emu-wren is listed as 'Endangered'. It was believed that the population in South Australia had become extinct so recently scientists have reintroduced a population from Victoria into South Australia. Hopefully, this new population will act as a safeguard should a fire destroy the habitat of the Victorian birds.

Eastern Curlew
Numenius madagascariensis
SHOALHAVEN HEADS, NEW SOUTH WALES

A species that has suffered a drastic decline of up to 80 per cent of its population in the last 30 years and is now listed as 'Critically Endangered'. This is mainly due to habitat destruction in the form of land reclamation of intertidal mudflats both in the Yellow Sea and Australia. All migratory waders require fuel in the form of food to migrate thousands of kilometres each year to breed. When humans remove these feeding grounds the birds cannot get the fuel they need, and they often starve and die. Unbelievably Australia continues with development within these important feeding areas, placing even more pressure on shorebirds including this species.

Regent Honeyeater
Anthochaera phrygia
NOWRA, NEW SOUTH WALES

The striking Regent Honeyeater is in dire straits with only an estimated 500 birds remaining in the wild. It is now classified as 'Critically Endangered'. If any species highlights the danger of removing large tracts of native bushland, it is the Regent Honeyeater. This species is wide-ranging, traveling from north-east Victoria to northern New South Wales in search of flowering eucalypts. Due to the loss, fragmentation and degradation of habitat its numbers have continued to slide until the species is now on the brink of extinction. Thankfully, people power has come to its aid with many contributing to an active recovery mission. With intensive tree plantings and a captive-breeding program, there is hope for this unique species.

Hooded Plover

Thinornis cucullatus

ULLADULLA, NEW SOUTH WALES

This attractive bird, with its black hood and red eye-ring, is a welcome sight at beaches around the southern parts of the country. Unfortunately, it has suffered a significant decline in numbers and is now listed as 'Vulnerable'. This is largely due to the disturbance humans create with their vehicles, dogs and horses on the sandy beaches, leading the birds to abandon nests. Hooded Plovers evolved to breed on the many coastal banks and sand bars surrounding Australia. Traditionally such places supported few predators, but today the birds are now prone to attack from introduced dogs, foxes and cats. Thankfully there is a large network of volunteers working tirelessly during the breeding season to help protect the birds and their young.

Great Knot
Calidris tenuirostris
SHOALHAVEN HEADS, NEW SOUTH WALES

The Great Knot is another migratory shorebird that has suffered a large decline
in numbers over the last 30 years and is currently classified as 'Endangered'.
Like the Red Knot and Eastern Curlew it faces the threats of land reclamation
and degradation of habitat. These shorebirds appear to be very loyal to particular
feeding areas, often returning to the same location year after year. When those areas
are reclaimed or destroyed, the birds do not appear very well adapted to finding
alternatives. This has led to a dramatic decline in numbers that does not appear
to be reversing or even slowing down.

Painted Honeyeater
Grantiella picta
CENTRAL COAST, NEW SOUTH WALES

The Painted Honeyeater is a nomadic traveler of coastal and inland eastern Australia. It has evolved to feed predominantly on the mistletoe berry which grows on eucalypts and acacia trees. They will often breed when enough berries are available. Like many species, the major threat is habitat loss and fragmentation. Due to their heavy reliance on mistletoe, any removal of host trees reduces the amount of available food. The species is currently listed as 'Vulnerable'.

Orange-bellied Parrot
Neophema chrysogaster
MELALEUCA, TASMANIA

The species most at risk of extinction in Australia is the Orange-bellied Parrot. Listed as 'Critically Endangered' and with less than 50 individuals left in the wild, this bird has become reliant on human intervention for its survival. The Orange-bellied Parrot is a migratory species which breeds in south-west Tasmania before migrating across the Bass Strait to the Australian mainland. It is not clearly understood exactly why their numbers have plummeted, however habitat loss and the arduous migration journey are two likely factors. With a captive-bred population and new funding from the Tasmanian government, there is hope that this species may one day recover.

WETLANDS

While Australia is known as the arid continent, it also has some of the most biodiverse wetlands in the world. From the wet tropics in the north to the salt lakes in the south, Australia has vast wetlands supporting enormous amounts of birdlife. This chapter showcases some of the birds which live in these habitats.

Black Swan

Cygnus atratus

PYREE, NEW SOUTH WALES

The Black Swan is the epitome of beauty in the bird world. This very large waterbird frequents most wetlands in Australia and is often seen in pairs or in large flocks. The birds often make a lot of noise, honking to each other when danger approaches. When they decide to fly they require a large run-up, flapping their wings to get airborne. Seeing a large flock of swans take off really is an incredible sight.

Australian Pelican
Pelecanus conspicillatus
LAKE WOLLUMBOOLA, NEW SOUTH WALES
This iconic Australian species is found across the continent wherever suitable

habitat exists. Its very large bill is well suited to catching fish and is believed to be very sensitive, allowing the bird to feel its prey in murky water. This species can feed alone, however it is often seen in small flocks. It is known to be a cooperative hunter and when there is ample food the flocks can become quite large.

Sacred Kingfisher
Todiramphus sanctus
WARBY RANGES, VICTORIA

A common sight at any large wetland are kingfishers perched on branches scanning the water and surrounding land for prey, although the Sacred Kingfisher usually favours invertebrates and reptiles rather than fish. It is the most common medium-sized kingfisher in Australia and can be found all over the continent, with some of the more southerly breeders heading north in winter.

Pink-eared Duck
Malacorhynchus membranaceus
BAMARANG, NEW SOUTH WALES

One of Australia's unique ducks is the amazing Pink-eared Duck. This species has a remarkable bill shape that is different from all other ducks in Australia. They also have interesting zebra-like striped patterns in their plumage and of course the small dash of pink behind the eye. Pink-eared Ducks prefer shallow lakes and swamps and can be found at most wastewater treatment plants – locations which appear to provide the perfect habitat for this species.

Red-necked Avocet
Recurvirostra novaehollandiae
LAKE WOLLUMBOOLA, NEW SOUTH WALES

This endemic species is unique among the shorebirds found in Australia, with its long legs, red head and a upcurved bill giving it unmistakable identification features. Avocets are found in shallow wetlands and tidal flats around Australia, frequently forming large feeding flocks. They can often be seen walking, sweeping their bill from side to side, sifting through the mud in search of prey.

White-headed Stilt
Himantopus leucocephalus
LAKE WOLLUMBOOLA, NEW SOUTH WALES

The beauty of wetlands is often the serenity of watching nature unfold in front of you. Photographing birds feeding can often present amazing opportunities. These two White-headed Stilts were feeding in unison one morning before sunrise. They came together and almost mirrored each other's behaviour for this photograph.

Grey Teal
Anas gracilis
SOUTH NOWRA, NEW SOUTH WALES

A common species of duck which inhabits a range of wetlands throughout Australia. They can be nomadic, moving from wetland to wetland in search of food. Unlike the Chestnut Teal there is no sexual dimorphism, with the male and female appearing identical.

Chestnut Teal

Anas castanea

SOUTH NOWRA, NEW SOUTH WALES

A widespread species of duck in eastern, southern and south-western Australia.
The male has a striking green iridescent head that gleams in direct sunlight.
The female is pale brown and is easily mistaken for a Grey Teal, which is slightly
lighter in colour with a paler throat. This species can be commonly encountered
on town lakes.

Broad-billed Flycatcher
Myiagra ruficollis
FOGG DAM, NORTHERN TERRITORY

Inhabiting large billabongs and coastal areas of northern Australia, the Broad-billed
Flycatcher gleans insects from the vegetation and can be seen perched on waterlily
seed pods and paperbark trees that line wetlands.

Royal Spoonbill
Platalea regia
LAKE WOLLUMBOOLA, NEW SOUTH WALES

One of two species of spoonbill found in Australia and easily identified thanks to
its distinctive black bill. This bird is found in most wetlands including estuarine
habitats. It often feeds in small flocks and when in breeding plumage the male
sports wonderful streamers on the back of its head.

Red-necked Stint

Calidris ruficollis

LAKE WOLLUMBOOLA, NEW SOUTH WALES

Rarely when photographing birds do you get perfect weather. The author was fortunate to experience such conditions early one morning. The water was like glass and the birds were busy feeding in the shallows. This stint's every move created small ripples and the bird's image was beautifully reflected in the water for this shot.

Comb-crested Jacana
Irediparra gallinacea
FOGG DAM, NORTHERN TERRITORY

Australia's only jacana is found in the north and north-east of the country. It has
evolved enormous toes which it spreads wide over lily pads to disperse its weight.
These birds can be found in most wetlands that support an abundance of lily pads.
Be mindful when visiting wetlands to view this species, as jacanas often share the
water with crocodiles.

NATURE'S PALETTE

One of nature's marvels is the truly remarkable array of colours and patterns found in birds. From the cyans and ultramarines of the fairy-wrens to the magenta of the Pink Robin's breast, Australia has every colour covered. This chapter showcases some of the incredibly coloured birds that call Australia home.

Common Bronzewing
Phaps chalcoptera
CALLALA BAY, NEW SOUTH WALES

The wing-feathers of the Common Bronzewing are remarkable, showcasing metallic greens and oranges which change colour in direct sunlight. The wings sparkle in the sunlight, which adds to the beauty of this species.

Scarlet Honeyeater
Myzomela sanguinolenta
VINCENTIA, NEW SOUTH WALES

The diminutive male Scarlet Honeyeater has the most vibrant red upper body which contrasts well with its black wings. This bird feeds on the nectar of many colourful native plants. One such plant is the Callistemon shrub, the flowers of which stunningly have the same vibrant red as the bird.

Pink Robin

Petroica rodinogaster

HOBART, TASMANIA

One of Australia's prettiest birds, with a breast so pink that some people can barely
believe it is real. How and why this bird acquired fluorescent highlighter pink for its
breast colour is a mystery. Australia boasts an array of beautifully coloured robins,
with the Pink Robin being high on the list of the most attractive.

Red-capped Robin
Petroica goodenovii
EULO, QUEENSLAND

Another very bright and colourful species. This small bird inhabits dry woodland
areas of Australia and has a lovely call. The male has a bright red breast and cap
which make it really stand out in the bush.

Regent Parrot

Polytelis anthopeplus

HATTAH, VICTORIA

One of the most stunning-looking parrots in Australia, with the bright yellow
plumage, red bill and touches of red on the wings making this a very attractive
species. This bird is uncommon and found in Mallee-type habitat in north-west
Victoria and south-west Western Australia.

Rainbow Lorikeet
Trichoglossus moluccanus
CALLALA BAY, NEW SOUTH WALES

Probably the most common parrot species in Australia, the Rainbow Lorikeet can be found along the east coast and has become abundant in many cities and towns that have native flowering plants. It is easy to see how this bird got its name with a rainbow of colours throughout its plumage making it stunningly colourful.

Zebra Finch
Taeniopygia castanotis
BOULIA, QUEENSLAND

It is easy to see how this bird got its name with zebra-style stripes adorning its upper breast and throat. It also sports bronze cheeks and flanks with a bright orange bill making this little finch really stand out.

Rainbow Bee-eater
Merops ornatus
SEVENTEEN SEVENTY, QUEENSLAND

Australia's only bee-eater and what a colourful bird it is. The golden-yellow head
and pale aquamarine body complement each other perfectly. It is always a marvel
how birds' colours can be so beautiful.

Australian Ringneck
Barnardius zonarius
GLUEPOT RESERVE, SOUTH AUSTRALIA

This remarkable species is widespread in the drier areas of Australia. It has four recognised subspecies which vary greatly from one another. The Mallee Ringneck subspecies featured here is a Mallee habitat specialist. Its plumage displays soft pastel shades in an array of greens, blues and yellows.

Flame Robin
Petroica phoenicea
WARBY RANGES, VICTORIA

Yet another striking robin with a colourful breast. This time it is the aptly named
Flame Robin showcasing a breast of bright orange. This species can form large
feeding flocks of up to 20 birds at a time. They are often seen in open forest areas
moving around on the ground.

Mulga Parrot

Psephotus varius

GLUEPOT RESERVE, SOUTH AUSTRALIA

With its fiery red 'trouser legs' and aqua green body, the Mulga Parrot is a bright
addition to outback Australia. The female is not as colourful as the male but still
shows a variety of colour in her plumage.

Splendid Fairy-wren
Malurus splendens
ROUND HILL, NEW SOUTH WALES

Splendid by name and splendid by colour, this all-blue fairy-wren is a gem of the
bush and one of Australia's most-loved bird species. The fact that its plumage
comprises a few different shades of blue adds to its natural beauty.

Crimson Rosella
Platycercus elegans
BANGALEE, NEW SOUTH WALES

The stunning Crimson Rosella displays beautiful red-and-blue plumage.
When the bird is young it has some green feathers, but these soon moult away
as the bird reaches adulthood.

Eastern Rosella

Platycercus eximius

WARBY RANGES, VICTORIA

Australia is often referred to as the land of parrots, with 56 different species recorded. Parrots are also some of the most colourful bird species on the planet, with the Eastern Rosella being one of the most impressive. Its plumage is a rainbow of colour and is a magnificent sight.

Regent Bowerbird
Sericulus chrysocephalus
CENTRAL COAST, NEW SOUTH WALES

One of the most striking birds in Australia with its incredible bright yellow and
black plumage. The yellow bill and eye also add to the overall impact, making this
bird really stand out.

Index by common name

Index by Latin name

Tragically author **Matthew Jones** passed away in 2018 and the preparation of this book was completed by his wife Nathaly and fellow author Duade Paton. Matthew was a wildlife photographer from Nowra, NSW. His work featured in the prestigious Australian Geographic Nature Photographer of the Year catalogue for three consecutive years. His background was in ecology, protected area management and nature tour guiding.

Duade Paton from Wangaratta, Victoria, has been an avid bird photographer for more than a decade and has seen his work nominated for various awards and feature in numerous publications including books and national newspapers.

Page 1:

Splendid Fairy-wren
Malurus splendens
HATTAH, VICTORIA

One of the most striking birds in the Aussie bush is the aptly named Splendid Fairy-wren. Its bright blue plumage contrasts starkly with the orange-brown tones of the outback. In eastern Australia it is synonymous with dry inland habitat including the Mallee in South Australia and north-western Victoria. In Western Australia it can occur at the coast in heath-type habitat. There are four subspecies with some having distinctly different plumage. The western subspecies *splendens* is a very dark shade of blue that almost appears violet.